How to increase
Sales
using Facebook.

Claretta T. Pam

Claretta T. Pam

How to increase sales using

Claretta T. Pam

How to increase sales using Facebook.
Entrepreneurial Universe Series (Volume 1)

Help Us Keep This Guide Up to Date

Every effort has been made by the author and editors to make this guide as accurate and useful as possible. However, many changes can occur after a guide is published.
We would like to hear from you concerning your experiences with this guide and how you feel it could be improved and be kept up to date. While we may not be able to respond to all comments and suggestions, we'll take all correspondence to heart and make certain to share them with the author. Please send your comments and suggestions to the following address:

Innovative Publishers Inc.
Double Click Press
Book ID #4705107
PO Box 300446
Boston, MA 02130

or you may email us at corrections@innovative-publishers.com

Cover art and design provided by
Taylor Pam – Fine Art LLC

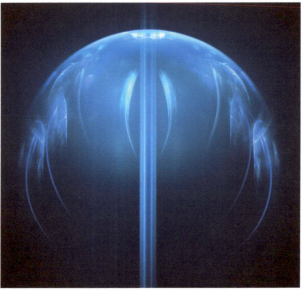

Art available for purchase at
http://taylorpam.artistwebsites.com/featured/fractal-142-taylor-pam.html

How to increase sales using Facebook

Copyright © 2014 by Claretta Pam

Innovative Publishers, Inc. & Double Click Press and colophon are trademarks of Open Nebula LLC, Intellectual Property Series.

Published and printed in the United States by
Innovative Publishers, Inc., Boston, Massachusetts

Innovative Publishers

Double Click Press

ISBN-10: 1-4913-2358-2   ISBN-13: 978-1-4913-2358-8 Paperback

Claretta T. Pam

ISBN-10: 1-4913-2363-9   ISBN-13: 978-1-4913-2363-2 Hardback
ISBN-10: 1-4913-2368-X   ISBN-13: 978-1-4913-2368-7 Kindle
ISBN-10: 1-4913-2373-6   ISBN-13: 978-1-4913-2373-1 iBook
ISBN-10: 1-4913-2383-3   ISBN-13: 978-1-4913-2383-0 Nook
ISBN-10: 1-4913-2378-7   ISBN-13: 978-1-4913-2378-6 AudioBook

Library of Congress Cataloging-in-Publication Data

Pam, Claretta T., 1969-
    How to increase sales using Facebook / Claretta T. Pam. -- 1st ed.
        pages cm. -- (Entrepreneurial universe ; Volume 1)
    ISBN 978-1-4913-2358-8 (pbk.) -- ISBN 978-1-4913-2363-2 (hb) --
ISBN
· 978-1-4913-2368-7 (ebook) -- ISBN 978-1-4913-2373-1 (ebook) -- ISBN
978-1-4913-2383-0 (ebook) -- ISBN 978-1-4913-2378-6 (audiobook)
    1. Electronic commerce. 2. Web site development. 3. Facebook
(Electronic
resource) I. Title.
    HF5548.32.P35597 2014
    658.8'72--dc23

10 9 8 7 6 5 4 3 2 1   14 15 16 17 18

An interpretation of the printing code: is the number of the books printing. The rightmost number of the
second series of numbers is the year of the books printing. For example, a printing code of 1–14 shows that
the first printing occurred in 2014.

First edition. June 2014

For general information on our other products and services or for technical support, please contact our technical support within the United States at admin@innovative-publishers.com online at http://innovative-publishers.com.

Most Innovative Publishers Inc. books are available at special quantity discounts for bulk purchases first sales promotions, premiums, fundraising, or educational use. Special books, or book excerpts, can be created to fit specific needs. For details, email info@innovative-publishers.com.

Other Titles:

How to make money using Pinterest
How to make money using LinkedIn
How to make money using YouTube
How to make money using Twitter

DEDICATION

To the entrepreneur that meets the challenge to follow their dreams.

Table of Contents

ACKNOWLEDGMENTS

CHAPTER 1

Getting Started

What is Facebook all about?

One search on Google and you won't need to ask what Facebook is. One of the most popular social networks on the planet, Facebook has a reputation that precedes the website itself. With an insightful and interesting past, this social platform has surpassed all expectations and figures when it comes to fame and success with its target audience.

At the close of the 90s, the social networking industry was sparingly dotted with a few websites that, though famous, were unable to gather all internet users on one platform. These sites were used to connect with friends and family members living far because interaction through these platforms was quick, easy and cheap. Hence, social networking was more of a term that either only existed in theory or was only practiced in the physical world i.e. face to face.

The inception of Facebook was nothing less than extraordinary. Founded in 2004, it wouldn't be incorrect to say that the birth of this social forum was a brainwave that struck Mark Zuckerberg, then a student at Harvard University. In a dingy dorm room, together with four classmates, Zuckerberg put together the algorithms for a website that would take the online world by storm.

Initially limited to Harvard University students only, Facebook was a hit right from the start. It presented a very easy and hassle free way to connect with people, share files, pictures and data with them and at the same time, have some fun. As its popularity soared within the dorm walls, the website was expanded to included students from several Boston Universities.

As the trial run for the social forum proved successful, the website opened for use by high school students nationwide and in 2006; it was made available for anyone above the age of 13. Popularity of the social network knew no bounds. Practically every individual who had a valid email ID and passed the age criteria was registered on Facebook within minutes of its launch. Thanks to Zuckerberg and his brainchild, the era of virtual social networking had just begun.

So what is Facebook all about? Facebook is no longer just a website or social platform. Today, 10 years after its launch, it has become a way of life. From students to businessmen to housewives, just about everyone, all around the world, with the slightest need or interest in networking, and staying in touch, can be found on Facebook.

Since the website proved to be a very stable forum for interaction, Facebook attracted attention from business and marketing circles long ago. Observers began to notice that the reach and penetration this forum generated was far beyond that of any other social blog or website. So much so, that official company websites were often left behind in terms of the extent of connectivity and interaction that this particular social network provided.

Hence, in short, Facebook provides an opportunity to not only connect with friends and family, it also enables businessmen to make room for their brands and marketing campaigns in the online world where advertising clutter often renders marketing tricks useless. With an award winning forum like Facebook and the hundreds of innovative features on it, promoting and selling products and brands has become easier, efficient, productive and much more fulfilling.

If you are one such individual who aspires to start an online business or promote existing products and brands to the online community, Facebook is the place to start. The rest of the topics in this pamphlet will take you through the steps for building a Facebook presence and then positioning your brand in the minds of the audience through constant interaction.

Make an Account

The first step to make an appearance on Facebook is to register with the website. Since registration is open to anyone, with no prerequisites except age, signing up with the website is free and easy. Registration is a one-step process that includes Making an Account which can then be used to log in to the website.

Before you can make an account, you need to have a valid email address. This email address should be your primary ID that you use to send and receive emails because Facebook will send notifications to update you of any changes made to your account settings.

Next, you need to have a steady internet connection so that while you go through the verification steps one by one, you stay connected to the internet. In case, you get disconnected, you will have to start the procedure again.

The steps to be followed to make an account are easy. The following illustrations clarify each step further.

Step 1: Go to www.facebook.com. The first two blanks on the top are for users already registered on the website. As a first time user, you will concentrate on the blanks below the Sign Up heading. The details needed for signing up are easy: first and last name, email address, password, gender and date of birth.

Step 2: Choose the appropriate options from the drop down menus of Gender and Date of Birth. Once you have filled all the details, double-check them. Make sure you have typed the correct password and email address because as long as you are registered, these two are your personal details for the Facebook Account.

Step 3: When you have checked the details, click the green Sign Up button. Facebook will process the information provided and lead you to another page.

Step 4: In case there is a problem with one of the answers, for instance, you have misspelled your email address, an error will appear. Read the warning message and fill the details again to make the necessary corrections.

Step 5: If all information is processed successfully in the previous step, a new window will open. This is the verification stage. To make sure a human is creating the account and not a robot, Facebook requires every new user to go through thisthe verification process that takes less than a minute. The security check will have a word written in a slanted and titled font, which is quite hard to read. Read the instructions given above the word.

Step 6: Once you have identified the word, you will now have to plug it in a blank given towards the end. This security check, called CAPTCHA, ensures that Facebook isn't used for activities like spamming. Write the case-sensitive word in the blank, and hit Sign Up.

Step 7: Your very first Facebook account is ready to be used!

Setting Up Your Profile

Once your account has been set up and you are registered with Facebook, you can use the social forum as and when you want. To make your first appearance quite impressive, a tutorial on the website will help you set up the account with the relevant details.

On Facebook, people recognize you by your 'profile.' A profile is a collection of all your personal information that you want friends and family to see. An entire page has been dedicated for you to build a profile that is attractive, interesting and worth a few clicks by Facebook users!

The most important steps to set up your profile are:

Step 1: Once your registration is confirmed, Facebook will redirect you to this page. This is the first screenshot of the Profile Setting Stage. The three most important steps are given at the top.

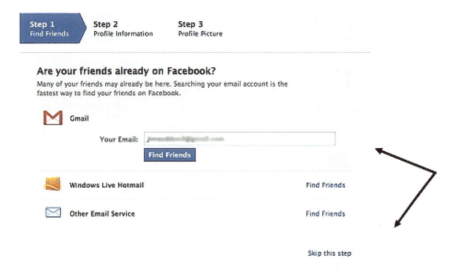

Step 2: Finding Friends who would view the profile is the first step. Facebook gives you the option to invite friends using your email address. Whether you have Gmail, Hotmail or any other email service, plug the email address in the space provided and click Find Friends. Make sure that this address is the same as the one you used to register with Facebook.

Step 3: Once entered, Facebook uses this email to access your contacts and find all those friends who are registered with Facebook. When the contacts are matched, friends are added using invitation requests.

Many users do not want to add friends in one go. Instead, they prefer adding friends manually so that they can pick and choose who views their profile. If you want to opt for manual addition, you can choose to 'Skip this step' as well.

Step 4: The next stage is Profile Information. Here, you get to add details like the name of the school you attended, work experience and the name of the employer/company. These details increase your visibility on the social network because many users search for friends and family members with filters like school, college, work or even profession.

As a first time user, you should consider adding all these details because you want to attract more and more people to your profile, which would eventually help build an audience for your online business.

Click 'Save & Continue' if you have filled in the boxes, or select 'skip' if you want to complete this step later.

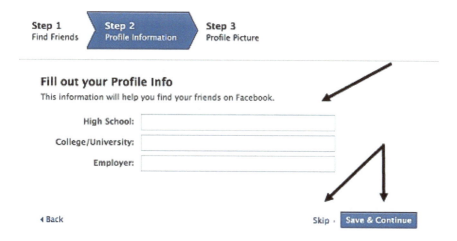

Step 5: The third stage of profile building is Setting a Profile Picture. On this page, you will have two options; you can either upload a previously saved photo from your computer or you can take a photo with your webcam to put up on Facebook.

The best way to familiarize yourself with others is to upload a picture of yourself. However, many people prefer to add pictures of their pets, sceneries or even famous celebrities. Either way, a good profile picture makes your personal details seem complete.

If you do not want to add this feature, you can also click 'skip.'

The About You page can be used for other personal details. It appears like this:

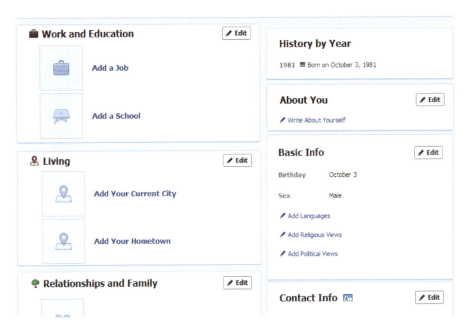

Step 6: Once all these stages are completed, you will be directed to a page that gives the view of your completed profile. At the top of this

page, you will read a verification message that asks you to select the option, 'Go to my email.' Click here. This option takes you to your Inbox where the Facebook team will send a verification email. Follow the instructions to start using Facebook and its fun features!

To make sure people visit your profile, try to personalize it as much as possible. Doing so increases the chances of being found on Facebook easily and it also makes for a profile that attracts a lot of attention, especially if you plan to do online business through your account. There are a number of ways to personalize a profile. Some of them include:

- Using a funny/attractive profile picture.
- Add famous quotes and sayings in the relevant section.
- In the biography section, put interesting details about your life, likes and dislikes and the general details regarding work.
- Update your marital status.
- Include your family members, hometown and any other details you want to share.

Because this is your personal page, it is really up to you how much detail you want to add and what to exclude. What should be remembered is that you want to invite people to visit your profile, like what they see and be willing to interact with for personal and business purposes.

CHAPTER 2

Facebook's Privacy Policy

Privacy Settings are an important consideration for all users on a social network. According to a survey, close to 13 million Facebook users have never even touched their privacy settings; hence, are unaware of what part of their profile, pictures and information others can view and share. Even though the website guarantees privacy, knowing how to limit or extend others the right to view your information is necessary.

Facebook's privacy policy is detailed on the website itself. According to the admin team, "We use the information we collect to provide our services and features to you, to measure and improve those services and features, and to provide you with customer support." Therefore, while the website has access to every piece of information you put up, it is only used to serve you better.

So while you may be hesitant to fill up most of the blanks given in the 'profile' and 'about you' pages, you can be assured that Facebook would be using the information only for the most meaningful purposes. Some of these include:

- Quality advertising: An aspect of the privacy policy of the website is targeted towards selective advertising. For instance, if you set up a profile with details that you run a business in the textile sector, Facebook uses this information to shortlist you for selected textile advertisements. These adverts are tailor made and personalized to spur interest in the receiver, demanding action.
- Friend suggestions: Depending on your interests and likes and dislikes, Facebook uses your personal information to make suggestions regarding friends, pages, social campaigns and other commercial events created by different users. These suggestions are filtered according to the interests you have.

- To supplement your profile: If you want to delete a picture, put a new one or ask a friend to un-tag you from a picture, Facebook needs access to your albums and personal information. Hence, to make sure your profile is as you want it to be, access to information is necessary.

Since privacy settings are so important, it is necessary to know how to set the appropriate ones for pictures, location, personal details and even the status updates that you will put up from time to time. The following are easy steps to change privacy settings.

Step 1: Go to your profile and spot the tab beside the security lock. Click on it and select Settings from the drop down menu.

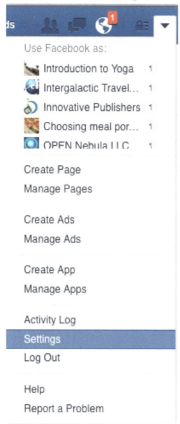

Click on 'Timeline and Tagging' on the left and then click 'View As' on the Who can see things on my timeline? Section. This option shows your own profile as seen by the public.

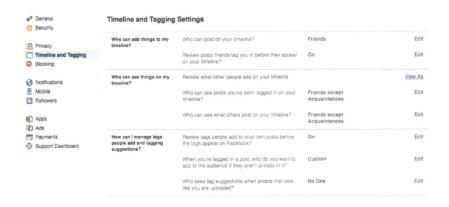

Step 2: When your profile appears, scan through it thoroughly. See what information and pictures are visible to the general public. Seeing your profile through the public's eye is helpful because it tells you what to hide and what to keep open to others. Therefore, this scanning phase is important for everyone who wants to limit their content to people close to them.

Step 3: From the previous step, make a note of everything you want to limit. Now click the cross sign to exit this mode.

Once you have decided which parts of your profile you want to limit, you can now start using Facebook's privacy options. For a quick privacy review, privacy shortcuts are also given on the top right corner of your Home Feed. This option is symbolized as a small lock beside the Profile banner. Some other detailed privacy options are:

Main Privacy Option

The main privacy option can be accessed under the settings sign that appears on the extreme right side on the News Feed page. Click on Settings, then choose Privacy from the options on the left.

Three main categories appear on this screen namely, 'who can see my stuff', 'who can contact me' and 'who can look me up.' Beside each option, an Edit sign is displayed; use it to change the settings as you want. Most privacy settings give options like Everyone, Friends, Friends of Friends, Custom and Only Me.

General Privacy

Under the cover photo, spot the About Me tab. On this page, you will see an Edit sign beside every category of personal information you have provided. Change these settings to enable or disable people from viewing your profile.

Use the follow button. The ability to be followed is a great method by which your visitors can keep track of your happenings on Facebook. You can control the privacy by restricting the followers to some extent.

Follower Comments: You can choose the audience that you require to be able to comment on your posts.

Follower Notifications: You can choose to receive notifications for the people who start following you but are not your friends.

Secure Browsing

You can secure your Facebook account through the secure browsing feature on Facebook. In order to make use of secure browsing (https) on Facebook, go to the account settings. Then choose the account security option and check the box "Secure Browsing (https)".

Pictures Privacy

Restricting everyone from viewing your personal pictures is one of the biggest concerns Facebook Users have. With regards to the pictures (excluding cover photos that are public by default), the website's privacy settings are quite elaborate; however, time, effort and understanding will be needed to make sure you have the perfect settings.

Album Settings: On your Profile, click on the Photos tab. Doing so displays your albums on one page. Under each album, click on the drop down menu to restrict it from being viewed.

Individual Photo Settings: Profile Pictures and Timeline Photos can only be restricted on an individual basis. Go to the picture you want to limit, click on Edit and select the appropriate option from the drop down menu.

CHAPTER 3

Making a Business Page

What is a Page?

It was previously discussed that Facebook is one of those social networks that can be used to conduct business, promote brands and post advertisements to market products. In short, a lot of promotional activities that were previously limited to the physical market are now conducted online with the help of special tools and features provided by Facebook.

One such tool is a Facebook Page. Such a Page is a platform provided by the website for businesses to promote themselves. One important function of pages, just like accounts, is to connect people and make them interact with each other. For a brand to have a Facebook Page, it needs to be very relevant to the audience it targets.

Because interaction is the key to promote a business, the Facebook Page feature has hit off considerably in the social world today. One search on the website and you will find thousands of pages being run by small and large organizations, all of whom want to increase their presence in the minds of the consumer.

Perhaps the biggest reason many established brands and companies have built interactive and interesting pages is that the audience on social networks like Facebook communicates in a very informal manner. Since the internet offers a high degree of anonymity, Facebook users feel comfortable voicing their honest opinions about brands and products that they may like or dislike. Keeping tabs on this impromptu feedback has proved beneficial and profitable for businesses.

Therefore, a page represents a business on Facebook. It can be customized and personalized to speak the language of the brand, to build similar associations as in the physical world and to depict the overall brand philosophy. Together with this, Facebook helps business owners manage pages well by connecting them to the main account; thereby, making it easy to post updates and keeping in touch with the online community.

As a business looking to build an online presence, a Facebook page can be of great value to your overall marketing strategy. The following sections explain how a page can be created and managed.

Information you need to get started

[insert worksheet]

Step-by-Step Guide to Making a Page

With the aim to market and promote a brand, the concept of a Facebook page seems daunting and making it feels like a hard task. However, making a Facebook page is quite similar to creating your very own profile. Just like you add a profile picture and put in personal details about work and life, a business page also begins with the same steps.

Unlike a profile, pages are visible to everyone registered on Facebook by default so that the maximum number of people get to like the page and promote it. A user gets access to pictures and details on a page by becoming a fan. This way, whenever you post an update about a product or a new launch, all fans are informed when the post appears on their News Feed.

Before you move on to making a Facebook Page, it is important to know that the website is quite vigilant against fake pages and spamming activities. All business pages are required to have authentic owners who are serious about promotion of the brand because in case of irregular activity, the page is deactivated by the team.

Following is a Step-by-Step guide to making a Facebook Page.

Step 1: Go to Facebook.com and sign in using your ID and Password.

Step 2: When you log in, you will automatically be directed to your News Feed. On the extreme top right corner, click the small circle that opens a drop down menu. Within the menu, click Create Page.

Step 3: When you land on the new window, you will see the following illustrations.

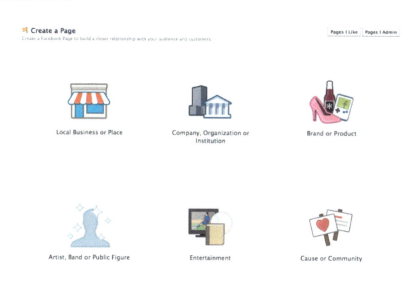

This is the first step to making a page for your brand. Here, you have to select what your page represents. Is it a page for a company, community, public figure or a brand?

Step 4: Click on the appropriate picture. Think before you do because this simple choice communicates the essence of your business to the audience and will appear on your page once it is completed. When you have made a choice, you will be prompted to choose a name for the page.

While this can be changed later, choosing a short and relevant name communicates strength and vision for the brand. Moreover, the same name also appears in the URL of the page; therefore, think of a name that represents the business precisely.

Step 5: With these easy steps you have created an official page to represent your business. At this point, the page would look like this:

Once you choose a name, Facebook will direct you to a window that will ask for further details about the page you have created. It is important to customize and personalize the page so that it appears attractive and interesting to the audience and is also differentiated from other pages at the same time.

Step 6: About: This step requires basic details about your business or brand. While you may edit the descriptions later, once people start liking the page, they should see appropriate information posted on it. Therefore, before filling out these blanks, think about the words you want to use to describe the page and the brand it represents.

If you have an official website, put the link on this page so that fans can be redirected to the website for further information about the business.

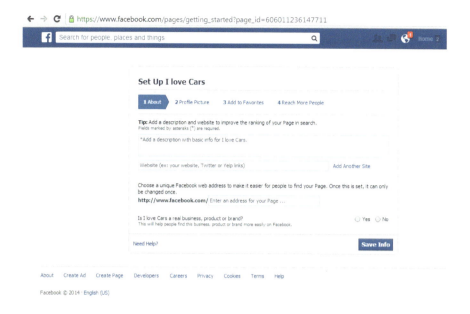

Step 7: Profile Picture: Fixed on the upper left corner, the Profile picture should represent what the page stands for. For instance, if the page is about cars, a picture of the best car you sell or its logo would be quite attractive. Every time you post an update from the page, this picture will appear on every fan's home feed. Therefore, make sure you select one that best speaks for the brand. This picture should be 180x180 pixels.

[insert screen shot of left side (favorites)]

Step 8: Add to Favorites: This option has been included to make access to the page easy and hassle free. When you add the page to your favorites, it will appear on the left column in your Home Page, making it easy to be reached anytime.

Step 9: Reach More People: The best way to reach more people is by making an Ad about the page. This Ad is managed by Facebook and circulated to all those who fall under the category you have defined as your target market. More detail about Advertising is given in the later sections.

Make Use of the Features

As more and more pages appeared on Facebook, the management of this website started to add advanced features to Pages to make it an ultimate marketing platform. To date, many new features have been added that have changed the outlook of a finished page that is ready to interact with its audience.

After complete customization, your page should look something like this:

1. **Admin Panel**: This area will be visible to the administrator/s. The page can be edited from here.
2. **Cover Image**: This is the main graphic that is going to be visible to your audience. Therefore, ensure that is eye-catching. The Facebook cover image needs to be 851×350 pixels.
3. **Profile Picture**: This profile picture represents you on Facebook. It should be around 180×180 pixels.
4. **Page Title**: The page title is the name of your Facebook Page. It can easily be updated whenever required.
5. **About Section**: This small area includes a concise sentence about what the page is about. This serves as the introduction of your page to the visitors.
6. **Timeline**: This area is where the main Facebook activity takes place. You can post information, notes, photos, events as well as videos.

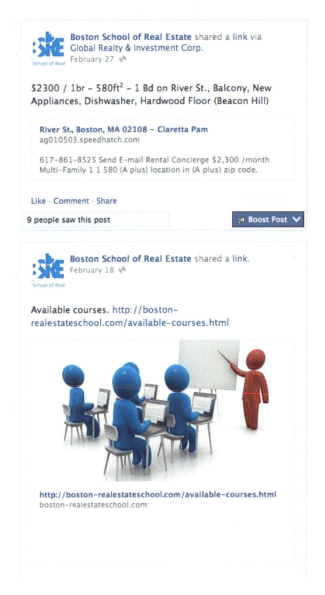

By using the features and guidelines proposed by Facebook, you can make your page one of the most liked ones in that particular category. What are these features and how can you use them?

Some noteworthy features are:

- Timeline photos and posts: When you have completed the Creation phase, you will land on the Timeline of your page. The timeline is used to post photos and updates about your business and to interact with the audience; spurring action and interest.

  The Timeline is like an open book. Whatever action you take, appears here and is then posted to the fans' News Feeds. Therefore, make sure you post and interact on the timeline on a regular basis.

- Pining: Pining is a relatively new feature added by Facebook. With this feature, page admins can pin or attach a particular post at the top of the page for several days to increase its visibility. For instance, if you have posted a new picture that you want to attract attention to, pin it to the top of the page. The Pin It option can be found under 'Edit.'

- Highlighting: Highlighting an update has a similar effect as Pinning it, i.e. it increases exposure and reach. You can highlight an important update by clicking on the star beside each post.

- Admin Panel: Perhaps, the best addition to the features for Facebook pages is the readily accessible admin panel at the top of your page. Only you and those you classify as Administrators of the page can view this section because it lets you control multiple features from one place. Information like notifications, messages, recent likes and insights for the page are all available for a quick glance.

- Cover Photo: Together with a profile picture, you can also add a cover photo to your page to make it more colorful, interesting and catchy. The cover photo goes at the top of the page and is usually the first thing a user sees when he lands on the page.

Therefore, choosing a cover photo with caution is quite necessary. Many administrators leave the cover photo option blank or fill it up randomly without much thought.

Doing so, however, is a mistake because the concept of Integrated Marketing suggests that every small cue about a business contributes to an image that is always remembered by the audience. Hence, treat the cover photo like a tool that adds a touch of creativity and glamour to the page.

- Invite Friends: Invite Friends is one of the most basic options on Facebook Pages. Invite friends and family members to like the page you have created to show support and encouragement. Because you have just started out, the more likes you get, the more credible you will seem to the internet audience.

- Invite Business Contacts: Even if your business contacts are not on Facebook, the website gives you an option to connect to them via email. You can make a list of all your contacts and send them an email, informing about the new page and inviting them to visit it. This feature is one of the most important and personalized ones for businesses who want to reach out to existing contacts.

- Share Post: The Share post option is useful to attract fans to your page. No doubt, to make this business page successful, you need people to interact with. Sharing the page on your Profile or that of a friend's is a good way to increase visibility and make people visit it. Therefore, whenever you feel you need more likes or simply want to remind people of your page, use the share option!

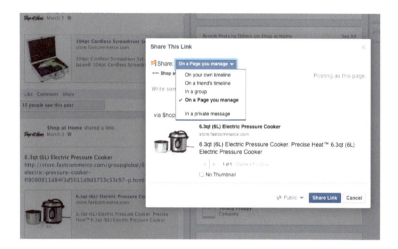

- Create Ad for target advertisement: To make online businesses popular, the feature Create Ads works like your very own ad agency! Details like the specifications of the target audience, the advertising budget, promotion timings, intervals and even the duration for which the ad should play can be chosen at will. The Create Ads feature is truly remarkable for businesses on Facebook to make use of the vast online community and penetrate further to increase presence, awareness and brand loyalty.

Advertise on Facebook

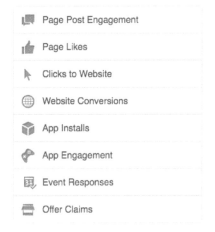

What kind of results do you want for your ads?

- Page Post Engagement
- Page Likes
- Clicks to Website
- Website Conversions
- App Installs
- App Engagement
- Event Responses
- Offer Claims

On the extreme right side of your page, spot the tab 'Promote Page' to make an advertisement and attract more fans.

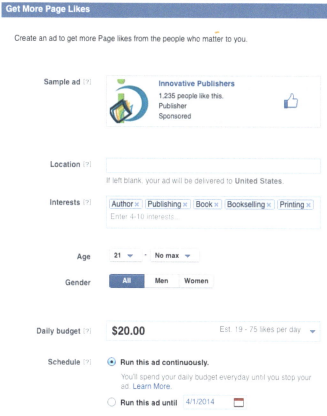

- Create Events: Just like a business holds events, parties and exhibitions physically, a 'Create Events' option lets online businesses inform fans about upcoming meetings, exhibitions and conferences. This option is present on the right corner of your page. Once clicked, it opens a new window where you can describe the event you want to hold, the time, venue, date etc. When you have specified these details, you can invite all the fans and send them a message regarding the event.

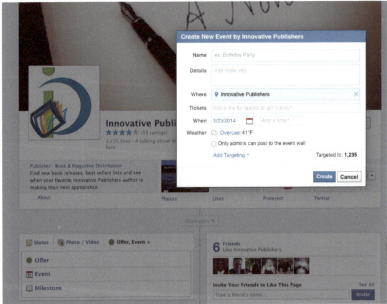

- Advertise particular posts: If you feel a particular post or update is receiving little attention, you can choose to promote it using the advertising feature. This means that apart from marketing the entire page, selected content can also be promoted to create awareness among the audience.

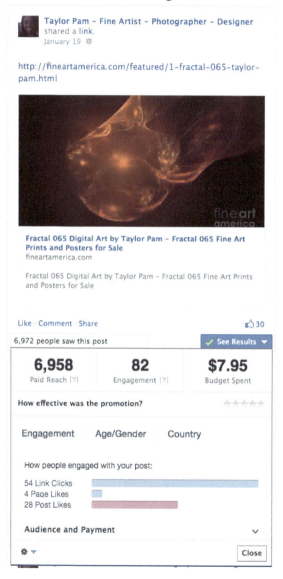

- Page Insights: Page Insights, a relatively new feature for Facebook pages, lets administrators see the progress they are making. Whether an advertisement generated likes, spurred interaction or increased the number of people talking about the page, every such statistic can be viewed and assessed from the Page Insights Features. This option also gives admins a road map for what to do in the future. If more likes are generated because of a marketing campaign, it signals to the team that ads are effective and should be used again in the future.

How to Manage Pages through a Master Account

Once you have created and customized your business page and understood all the features at your disposal, the next step is to manage the page. Management of a business page on Facebook is a 24/7 duty. Remember, the online community never sleeps, literally! Hence, you need to keep a watchful eye over every activity and interaction on your page. Who said what, how well was the response on an update and what did your fans feel about an upcoming event; all such information should be managed well by page administrators.

To make management of a page easy and hassle free, Facebook lets you be in charge of multiple pages with one master account. For instance, let's say you have registered on Facebook and made a profile for yourself. Next, you want to create and manage two business pages separately, under different names. Is that possible? Absolutely.

Following are some basic steps to start managing your pages from one account.

Step 1: Sign in to your Facebook account using your ID and Password.

Step 2: On the Home Feed, go to the top right corner where the small circle symbol is. Click on it for a drop down menu to appear. The first heading in the menu says 'Use Facebook as:' and underneath these words, all the pages that you have created with this account will be listed.

Step 3: Whichever page you want to manage, click on it. With this option, you can make changes, post pictures and update statuses as the page's administrator. Hence, whatever you do, instead of your name, the name of the page appears in News Feeds.

Step 4: When on that particular page, you can do a number of activities. Either reply to messages sent by fans, post new photos that spur interest or simply check the page's insights to see how well your online presence is. To make these admin roles easy, Facebook's page layouts are quite simple, enhancing visibility of some of the most used features.

The following Page for a new book is an excellent example of how the new Pages layout makes management quick and easy.

The timeline feature on the right gives a snapshot of when various activities happened. With different tabs for Photos, Map and Videos, admin can easily navigate to post updates and keep track of fan activity.

Very recently, Facebook launched an application called Facebook Pages Manager, which has been designed to manage pages efficiently via Smartphones. Available on iPhone, iPads and Androids, this application is quite handy for all page owners who want to manage their activity on the go.

6 Ways to Make Your Page More Attractive

The importance of having a Facebook page is immense today. With every business fighting for a share of the online community's attention, it is necessary to have a Facebook page where you can interact with your target audience, take advantage of selected advertising and implement the feedback given by the market.

However, keep in mind that not every Facebook Page sees success. While it may be easy to create a page, customize it and install the Pages App to monitor it 24/7, it is definitely not easy to be tactful, business-minded and smart when it comes to timing posts and updates and steering the direction of conversations.

Therefore, being complacent after creating a page is definitely not an option because there are many examples of businesses that fail to do well online because of lack of direction, vision and a web administrator team that knows the online market well. What can you do to make sure your page is successful and attracts your target market? Here are five tips to manage your business page better.

1. Constantly Interact: Most Facebook pages die because they are seen as tools to be used when your business is not doing well. Writing a post or two when your sales are low is not a solution to the problem. Constantly interact with the audience; tell them you are here for good!

2. Use Visuals: No one bothers to read long paragraphs or visit hyperlinks that have no thumbnails. Make sure you use lots of visuals wherever possible because relevant visuals induce life into page content.

3. Create a Brand Theme: As mentioned previously, an integrated marketing approach is essential to the success of a brand's page. Use similar colors, layout and themes that are associated with your brand when it appears offline.

4. Make Use of Features: Features such as highlighting and pinning may sound insignificant, but they play a huge role in attracting attention and making a business page look professional.

5. Post but Don't Overdo: Going overboard with posting is one of the biggest mistakes many novice admin members make. Posting updates once or twice, a day is good, but spamming News Feeds is not only unprofessional, it may also result in deactivation of your page by Facebook.

Set a Unique URL: A unique URL will always enhance your business image and will provide a professional appeal..

CHAPTER 4

Make the Most of Your Page

Develop a Strategy

For optimizing your online resources and garnering the largest audience on Facebook businesses have to strategize and come up with blueprints for their planned actions which would bolster their sales. A strategy would basically encompass all elements of your business plan and it should achieve the goal of increasing sales, increasing profits, expanding the market share or fortifying market power. The best way to plan a strategy is to start with a goal, assess the costs and benefits, and then to single-mindedly execute the plan. A back-up strategy should always be available if the current one fails.

Formulating Strategies

1. Goal: Having clear and achievable goals will be helpful in the first stage. By using Facebook analytics, gauge your present status and study the nature of your customer base so you can design strategies to market to the right people. You should carefully decide the number of fans, sales or likes you want to achieve and give yourself a timeframe. In addition it is important that the plan you devise aligns perfectly with the offers or advertisements on your website or physical outlet.

2. Organization: It is important to organize how the plan will be executed. Having a calendar to mark deadlines and important dates for posting content will help organize your strategy. This will also ensure that the plan follows the given period. You can include the topic and the timing of your post in your content calendar. An online spreadsheet or a calendar on a Personal Digital Assistant will help you keep track of your activities and keep your focus on the plan.

3. Action: Increasing the number of Facebook fans is the primary objective for increasing your sales. You will have a diversified base of consumers who will be viewing your posts and offers at different times of the day. Therefore, having a balanced and evenly placed sequence of posting updates will be beneficial. Ensure that the content posted is well-designed and informative so that users do not ignore it. Visualizing content is another great way to grab attention; diagrams, infographics, flowcharts and educational tidbits are well-liked.

Making a Strategy

There are several ways that you can channelize your resources to make the most of your Facebook page. Some of these common strategies are described as follows:

- For promotion of your Facebook page the most important thing your need is consistent viewership and consumer outreach, which means that the links to your Facebook page should be advertised along with your website URL or the physical location of your outlet. You can redirect the traffic from your website to your page by providing a social media icon on your website. Having the Facebook icon on the homepage and several other places on your website will mean that more potential visitors will click on it. On your business cards or in emails, include the link to your Facebook page so that people can easily follow it. Another strategy is to connect your offers to the Facebook page, for instance you can promote an offer by saying, 'get free gift by liking our Facebook page.'

- You can also use Facebook plugins on your website to promote your product or service. Providing users with the 'Like' or 'Share' option on your blog or webpage is one way to integrate your brand image. The Follow Button, Comments, Recommendations Bar, Send Button are other social plugins which can be used to advertise your content.

    o The primary social plugins are:

- Like button: used to connect with items from other websites that interest you.
- Share button: used to share and write a blurb about something that will then be posted on your website.
- Embedded posts: any public post from Facebook that you use on your blog or website.
- Comments box: used to publicly comment on another site using your personal Facebook account.

- Using Facebook ads will allow you to get new users for the page. Such a service is a wise investment, as ads appear in the newsfeed of potential customers as 'suggested posts' or appear on the sides of the homepage on Facebook.

- Another strategy could be to use your existing fans to bring in more fans. This can be done by having contests where users have to gather enough likes for their photos or posts. Giving prizes at the end will result in positive publicity for your brand.

A good Facebook page interacts with users, answering their queries, replying to questions or considering their suggestions. In addition you can involve users with the '@' symbol to tag them in the posts that you share.

CHAPTER 5

Get More Likes

Those who like a Facebook page, become fans of that product or service in the online realm. They will also receive updates and offers of the page in their daily newsfeed so that if they are interesting in buying or suggesting the page to other friends they can do so. Liking a page will link you to its activities. Having a reputable and interactive fan base on Facebook does not always mean that you have to buy 'likes'. Although buying likes is the easier approach that will garner you enough strength and market power, so that when new customers view your page the number of likes would serve as a form of credentials for the brand.

In reality, focusing on building a good and friendly customer base will take some time and effort. You can use one or all of the following options to get more likes on Facebook:

- Ads: Paying for ads on Facebook is one way you can direct potential fans towards your page. You can advertise your brand name, brand image or logo along with some offers or descriptions of your business. If the users are interested, the likelihood of them clicking on the ad and visiting your page increases. However, ads are merely a way to direct users, not to retain or increase their interest in a business.

- Content: Once a user visits your page, they will look for good content. Ensuring that they find something interesting, engaging or vibrant on the page is important. In addition, you should always remember that your existing fan base is the key to new likes; if you present users with good content it is likely that they will share it on their wall, like it, comment on it or tag their friends in the post. All this channels visitors to your page and your job is to work on informative and creative content for the users.

- Images: The use of lively and relevant images is very important. Investing in a good designer for different posters or brochures as well as strictly using images that promote the brand will help your users take your brand seriously. Images should not be irrelevant and you should focus on producing original work by using Photoshop or any other design tool so that you can place your watermark or brand logo on the image. This will serve as an instrument for advertising.

- Interesting Facts: No matter which industry you operate in there is always more to your brand and product than you are aware of. You can conduct researches into the background of your product or industry and provide users with fascinating new details which they would like to share with their friends. For this you can focus on history, current events or bizarre facts about the product.
- Promotional Apps: You can also incorporate different promotional apps on your Facebook page. You can have content, videos, coupons, quizzes, trivia, favorite picks on your page to allow your fans to participate in your business.
- Follow rules: Getting more likes is a marketing strategy and it will obviously require your undivided attention, along with adherence to some rules which would make this strategy effective. Staying consistent with your posts and evenly distributing contests will help involve your fans. In addition, it is essential to ensure that the content stays relevant to the page and that it is not shoddy, untruthful gimmicks.

Engage With Your Fans

Why is it Important to Interact?

Unlike a website, Facebook offers businesses the unique feature of being able to contact their customers as a group or even personally. Astute entrepreneurs will capitalize on this opportunity and build their relationship with the customers; in this way they will be able to decrease the detachment that results from interacting through online media. A Facebook page is much better than a website in terms of interaction because the user knows the administrator on the other end will promptly respond to their request or query.

The user also feels empowered because he or she can post on the wall of the page publically. As a business keen on presenting a good image, you should always respond to users so that it does not reflect badly on your brand name. This also means that you can provide good customer support to the users as well. A healthy one-on-one relationship with your customer base will allow you to learn more about their outlooks, habits and other demographic details which will help you customize your advertisements and offers to target the right people.

How to Interact

There are several ways you can optimize your strategy to engage fans.

1. Study the analytics of your Facebook page in order to understand how different metrics of your page vary per post. This will help you focus on activities which will increase fan participation and elicit more reactions, and it will let you know which activities to eliminate from your content.

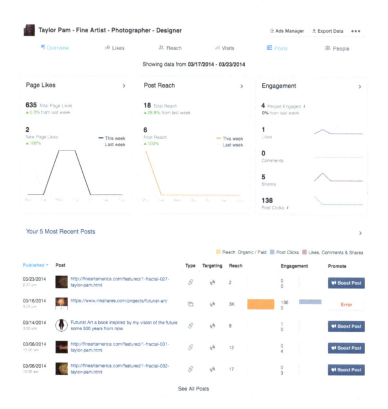

2. Focus on producing posts that maximize likes and observe the timings of your posts to gauge approximately when most of your fans are online. By promoting your page during peak hours you will be able to interact with the most people. If someone comments on a post or asks a question, be sure to reply to it instantly. In many cases, users will ask you a

particular question more than once and you should always answer it instead on relying on them to find the information themselves on the page. Use the insights section for your page to find out the likes, unlikes, paid likes and net likes per day:

Through this you can easily find out where the likes for your page and posts are coming from and then you can strategize to focus more on those customers.

3. Studying your fans, their location and habits will help you understand them better. You can tailor make the content so that it is suitable for your fans in particular. For instance, if you sell clothes for young people then your post should be catchy and vivacious. You can also focus on the particular geographical location, gender, age group and lifestyles of your fan base. You can use the 'people' tab to find out details about your fans, when your fans are online.

4. It is equally important to capitalize on the personal interaction feature Facebook provides to users. You should observe which fans on your page stand out and are more interested in the business. Focusing on these super fans will be beneficial in the long run because the positive publicity of your business will spread in the social circle of your super fans. This also creates a multiplier effect for the promotion of your brand and you can ask your fans to suggest changes which similar fans would be interested in.

5. Expand the reach of your posts by analyzing how many users view your content. Using the reach tab you will be able to see the graph for the popularity and viewership of your posts. It also shows you information like what amount of users disliked your page, reported your content or hid your posts. It will help you reevaluate the success of your strategies.

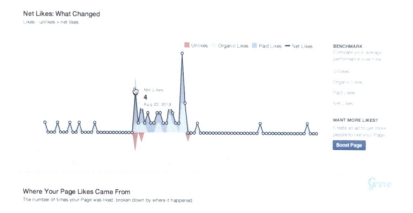

6. Schedule your posts on your Facebook page so that you can provide updates to your visitors without being online all the time. The Facebook scheduling option will help you post an update precisely when you require it to be visible by your visitors. You can also backdate your posts if you wish to. Scheduling your posts will allow you to plan ahead of time and get things done without having to wait.

Track Your Progress

Investing your time and energy in Facebook will yield positive results only if you objectively approach your strategies and follow through until the end. One of the most important facets of measuring success is evaluating your position at several points in time, during the execution of your strategy. For instance if you are engaging in posting updates on Facebook twice a day for a week, you should check your progress in the middle of the week and at the end of it. For a more aggressive evaluation, you can also do it daily, but the point is to keep a check on your progress.

The 'Insight' section in Facebook allows you to easily track your performance and review the success or failure of your strategy. The biggest advantage of such a reassessment is that it will inform you of failed strategies which you can then eliminate from your plan. Even if you are not directly selling products on Facebook, you can always create awareness about your brand name online and generate a presence in the market.

In broader terms, the number of likes, comments, likes per post, wall posts, messages in the inbox and number of times your post is shared will tell you where you stand in terms of your online viewership. The audience on Facebook is very large and diversified, therefore it is wise to track your progress. You will need different forms of statistical tools like graphs, pie charts, scatter plots to show you how successful your page is. There are broadly two ways to track your progress.

Firstly, you can use the page's Insights section by clicking **on Pages, click on page to view** and then **See Insights.** Through this, you can see how many people your post reached, how many people clicked it and how many people liked it, commented on it or shared it with their friends. From the **Reach** tab in this section, you can find out the number of viewers for the activity on your page. You can also find out the total **Likes, Comments** and **Shares.** For per post metrics go to the Posts tab.

In the tab **Overview**, you can view **People Engaged** for your page posts. This refers to people who have clicked on, liked, shared or commented on your wall posts. You can find out the **Engagement Rate** by going to the **Posts** tab, scrolling to the **All Posts Published** tab, selecting the drop menu of the option **Post Clicks / Likes, Comments & Shares** and lastly, clicking on Engagement Rate.

You can also find out the result of your investment in ads by looking at the Organic and Paid Reach. In addition to the Insights graph, you can find out the progress of your page on a daily basis. Dips and spikes in your progress are clearly delineated. By going to the **Visits** tab you can find out the number of views for your page and the external sources which are referring to your page.

This section intuitively guides you about the wrongs and rights of your strategy. For instance, in the **Post Types** tab you can find out which posts were most liked by viewers and from the **Hide, Report as Spam and Unlikes** section under the **Reach** tab, you can find out how many viewers you have lost. In some cases you can also view how other pages are performing and compare your progress to theirs.

The second way to review your performance is to use third party analytics software to interpret data for you in a meaningful form. Klout and PeerIndex are common social media analytics startups which measure the performance of your Facebook page and give you a score based on several kinds of variables. Klout uses variables like True Reach, number of engaged audience; Amplification, probability of the content being acted upon; and Network, influence of the engaged audience. PeerIndex uses the variables of Authority, Activity and Audience to give the page a score.

Make Your Page Discoverable

Increasing the viewership for your page is a feasible and achievable goal which businesses should focus on. It becomes a part of your promotion policy since you will have to ensure that your page is widely known on Facebook, in the search engines, and is referred to by other websites or blogs as well. This will give your page a wider audience as your posts will reach more people outside the Facebook community. There are a number of important variables which need to be considered for optimizing your Facebook fan page so that it can gain higher rankings in the search engine results.

The first component would be to have an intuitive and unique name which depicts the purpose and topic of your Facebook page. In most cases it will be your brand name or the name of the service that you are offering. If you are setting up a new business, brainstorm catchy and appropriate brand names for your business. Focus on the forte of your business or the industry in which you operate rather than choosing a name that is stuffed with keywords. It will be unlikely for a long and wordy name to be tagged in other areas on Facebook. Creativity is also important because generic names will not receive high rankings on the search engine.

You can also create your own Facebook URL or username which should be relevant to the purpose of your business because the default URL of your page is not SEO friendly.

Next, you have to focus on the Meta Description of your page which is simply the information you enter in the 'About' section of your page. Make sure that the information is well-phrased and written in Standard English, incorporates a few keywords and is succinct and pertinent to the business. The description should not be longer than 140 characters. You can also add other details like the mission statement or other product fields in this section. Adding your local address, country zip code and phone number will also allow your business to be indexed for local search results.

Introduction to meditation
26 likes · 3 talking about this

Book
Introduction to meditation is now available on amazon.com
https://www.createspace.com/4071491
Free in Kindle lending library.

You should incorporate keyword in the first 18 characters of your standard status update on Facebook. If you are posting the link to your page, you should enter the description for it in the 'say something about this link' text box. The first 18 characters of this too will appear in the SEO title.

It is also important to get more authority online by providing a link for your Facebook page on other platforms so that users are more likely to be redirected to your page. Adding the Facebook icon or link on your website, in a Twitter account, on a blog or other areas will help increase visibility for your page.

Similarly, the updates you post daily will be very important in determining your overall ranking, so try to make sure that the first word of your status update is a keyword. You can also provide links to your website and its pages when posting statuses, photos or other updates. This will divert more traffic to your website as well.

Whatever links or updates you post on your website have a separate page too. You can enter the main keyword in the comment box under the post and write the rest of the comment or descriptive lines about the post underneath it.

You can also optimize the notes on your Facebook page by using a SEO title with keywords. Use your notes to add detailed information about the service, the product, its history, milestones or any other in-depth information related to your business for which you do not want to redirect your users.

When posting photos, tag your page name in it so that it will appear in search results, this way in the graphic or image search in any search engine, your photos will have a higher chance of appearing in the top searches.

In most cases producing good quality content will make your page discoverable and popular.

CHAPTER 6

Promote Your Page

Share Diverse Content

The content of your Facebook page will be the primary factor that encourages people to visit your page or like your posts. Understanding your audience is very important for creating the right type of content. The insights of your page will give you the demographic details of your audience, i.e. their age, location, which will help you determine what kind of content is relevant.

The Facebook audience is composed of a wide variety of people from different backgrounds, education levels, interests, lifestyles and life experiences so you have to make sure whatever you post or share is specific to your business, but at the same time, can accommodate the interests of a diverse audience. Your page should be a refreshing blend of information and entertainment, which means that you will have to deliver content in a brief yet powerful way.

Information: Not all the content you post needs to be dry or filled with facts. Information overload will usually discourage users from reading anything and since you have only the first few seconds to make an impact on the reader make sure you make the content worth their while. Organize content in the form of lists or tips so that it is easy to browse through. Secondly, make the opening line attention grabbing for the readers. Make sure all your information is accurate and up-to-date.

Entertainment: Interesting posts always garner the most attention and this includes comic memes, photos, short videos, comics, infographics or any other form of visual aid to entertain the audience. Jokes or bizarre facts are well-liked by all types of people. At the same time you can make information visual by posting educational photos.

Local Flavor: If you are operating in a certain area, you will want to focus on the outlook of the residents of that area, changes in language, local traditions, customs, national holidays and other types of celebrations that will allow your audience to feel an affinity with the admins of the page.

Neutral Tone: If you are catering to a large number of users who belong to different places, religions or cultures, then as a business your purpose is to remain strictly neutral and prevent your prejudices or biases from seeping into the content. If a statement issued on the official page of a business sparks controversy, it will reflect badly on the brand as a whole.

Expand: Operating in a particular industry does not mean you only have to post content strictly relevant to it. You can always look into other areas of knowledge users might be interested in. For instance, if you have a page about baked goods then you can look into nutritional values of different food, dietary plans, healthy living, and history of the ingredients you use, fitness and exercise or even something as unique as dining table etiquette. Although all these topics are not related to baked goods directly, they introduce an edge to your Facebook page and your fans will not feel like they are being fed monotonous information.

In essence, brainstorming various areas or themes of the industry in which you operate will keep users engaged. You should always balance the factual and the fun side of your work so that the users can relate to the product or service. This way they will be more likely to share it on the walls of their friends or relatives with similar interests.

Tell Your Story

Perhaps the best part about having a business on Facebook is that it is more interactive compared to a website, but still gives owners the liberty of running an e-store without the problems of a typical retail shop. Websites largely face this problem because the entire communication is one way and the user feels disconnected from the business. Even if customer support is available, they are not likely to use it. Facebook provides a community within which a business can operate. The aura of friendliness and connectivity on Facebook is stronger for several reasons.

There is an entire community of fans, which can interact with each other based on shared interests and put forward their opinions by posting on the wall of the page. If they have some queries or are facing problems, they can always communicate with another customer. Customers can help each other out and provide relevant information when the admin of the page is not available.

Secondly, an important factor is that the admin of the page is always a message away. This gives users great confidence in conducting transactions and asking questions about the product because the admin is within their reach. They do not feel disconnected while posting on the page or communicating with the admin because they feel connected to a community.

Therefore, it is important for you to revamp your business ideology and interact with your fan base by allowing them to feel like a part of the business. A business is the brainchild of the business owner after all, so there is great motivation for personalizing your Facebook page, in order for it to tell the users your story and allow them to feel connected to your plans.

When telling your story, focus on the truth and creatively reconstruct your own journey and theory behind the business. Your story does not have to come in form of a lengthy note; you can use several wall posts to create a timeline of your business and its achievements. You can include photographs of important events or tag other people who may have contributed to your success. The best method of telling the business story is to talk about how it all began, its historical roots, the teams responsible for its success and so on.

An inspiring and motivational story holds more resonance for the audience because they will be interested in knowing how a certain brand came to be what it is. Oftentimes they can relate to the story or even be motivated by it to initiate some project in their own lives.

Overcoming hurdles is another interesting aspect of your story, because businesses are usually seen as profit maximizing ogres. You can shift this paradigm by telling the fans about any obstacles you faced or are facing currently. If you operate a business that focuses on creativity and you want to generate new ideas, the best way to do so is to simply ask your fans for suggestions. This will give you an idea about their expectations and you will not have to do any market research to know what to produce. Involving fans in the running of your business makes them feel connected and related.

You can use the Events tab on your page to earmark any significant milestones or achievements in the lifespan of the business. Similarly you can create custom tabs to list case studies, customer testimonials, product details, videos, etc. Making a photo album of your daily progress will also inform fans of your journey, chronologically. You can organize the albums by dates and give them catchy titles so that users could follow your business story.

Promote Affiliates and Other Businesses

Your business on Facebook is part of a large community of people and businesses in a similar industry. Most businesses follow the rules of competition and the aim is to maximize profit generally, but on Facebook building a good reputation and investing in goodwill is equally essential. A business on Facebook has to function as a socially responsible agent, which is well-linked to different, similar businesses or individuals with similar interests.

Businesses do not function in isolation, and several parties and stakeholders have a vested interest in the way a business operates. On Facebook, businesses can improve their PR by interacting with affiliates, sponsors or other businesses. Businesses that are affiliated with large corporations or sponsored by corporate giants greatly benefit from promoting their sponsors and affiliates because they can tap into the audiences and fan pages of those sponsors.

This is a mutually beneficial arrangement because the sponsor also benefits from being able to advertise to the fan base of the business. The users become more aware of the links a particular business has and it will greatly increase the credibility of your business if it is endorsed by a well-known brand or sponsor.

You can also promote individuals on your page, which will add a human element to your business because fans will be able to see the people in charge. This in return benefits the business because the associates will be eager to promote the business on their own profiles and their friends can also view the page. Publically acknowledging the efforts, hard work and contribution of your associates will highly motivate them.

Publicizing your affiliate products is also beneficial because it will help redirect traffic towards the original website and you can obtain updated content from the website to post directly on your wall. This will give your page credibility and the website will benefit from increased visibility.

Similarly, there will be hundreds of other businesses, similar or different, which will be tapping into the same customer base. Users on Facebook have great liberty to switch their preferences for brands, therefore it is in your interest to promote a similar business once in a while. This will spark a need for reciprocity and out of courtesy the said business will also promote your page.

Such an advantageous arrangement is rarely available to stores. Interaction of different businesses on Facebook in such a manner creates an atmosphere of camaraderie such that possibilities for integration, joint ventures, joint advertising and social networking arise. You can promote businesses that inspire you, businesses of friends or relatives, or businesses in which you have a corporate interest. Ultimately, it increases the chances for endorsements by different brands or individuals, which is a highly advantageous prospect for your business.

Tagging them in your posts, sharing their photos or updates, liking their page, or adding links to their website on your page will allow the business to take notice of your efforts. Browsing through the content of similar businesses will indirectly inform you about the level of competition and what tools you can incorporate on your own page to increase viewership.

Offer Deals

Keeping your fans involved and excited is a crucial element of the success of your Facebook page. The fan base on Facebook will be wide and diverse and in order to keep them engaged, you need to devise creative ways for them to participate in the business. In order to increase sales and popularity, the easiest thing to do is to offer deals so that fans can participate and inadvertently promote your page. Deals usually incentivize customers to purchase items in bulk or to participate in some other activity in return for a prize.

Landing page: Reflect your deals through a landing page. The landing page created to promote the deals will set the stage for your visitors. It will instantly provide a sense of professionalism and will make the visitors feel valued. Though a clean and simple landing page can do the trick, a flashy video can instantly grab user attention.

Indirect Deals: In this category, deals that are offered by your physical outlet can be publicized on your page so that your fan base can be informed about the new offers. You can indirectly divert your fan base towards your outlet. This would include 'buy one get one free' deals or other types of special offers available at the outlet.

Direct Deals: These are deals offered directly on the Facebook page and by following the requirements, users can claim prizes or obtain the product packages at discounted rates. The deals are available exclusively to the fan base and exist for a limited time. Usually such deals are offered on holidays or other celebratory occasions. In a deal, you basically combine more than one product to make a package and offer it at a certain rate.

Competitions: Competitions are a refreshing new way to involve fans and increase likes on your Facebook page. You have to devise a writing contest, photography competition or any other type of competition where users have to share their original work on the page. Either the admins judge it themselves and choose a winner or the winner is chosen based on the number of likes their work gets. This leads to unpaid publicity on a large scale for the business. In some contests, the admin might award the most active fan with a bonus gift in order to encourage more activity on the page. A business can collaborate with another business to sponsor the prizes for the contest.

Exclusive Discounts: These are reduced price offers available exclusively for Facebook members. You can offer coupons to users which they can redeem and use.

Facebook Offers: Similar to exclusive discounts, you can create Facebook offers for your products, which expire after a certain time. However, businesses that are categorized as local businesses will be able to provide these offers.

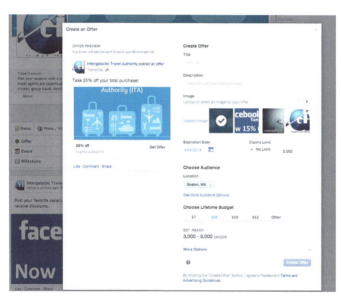

You can get the offer and an email will be sent to your account, which can then be printed and shown at the outlet to get the discount or free product. A typical offer includes a headline, an image, the redemption limit, the expiration date, and other terms and conditions of the offer.

Advertise on Facebook

Advertising on Facebook will get your brand more attention from diversified sources. However, you need to ensure that your page has optimized its content and can attract enough users on its own. You can use a Facebook badge. A Facebook badge offers your business the opportunity to promote and advertise the page outside of Facebook. It serves as a direct link that helps bring customers towards your Facebook page.

In order to procure more response from the Facebook community you can also modify the quality of the content you post. Aim to shorten the length of your posts and increase the frequency of updates so that you can reach wider audiences. Relying on organic reach that is viewership by the existing fan base can slow down the promotion process because advertising is not that aggressive and you might not be able to uniformly reach all of your fans at once. Therefore, paid advertising helps boost online visibility for Facebook pages.

Collect Information

The first step in order to create an ad on Facebook is to gather sufficient information to make your ad appealing and informative. Link back your advertising plan with your business plan and carefully think about the service or product you wish to promote. If you are promoting an affiliate product make sure you include a link to the website in the ad. If it is an event, mention the venue, time, date and other details to facilitate potential attendees. Personalizing your ad is also important and this can be done by adding your brand logo or the poster for the event.

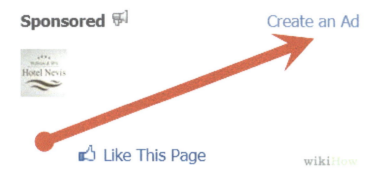

Deciding the Purpose of the Ad

A Facebook ad can serve several purposes and you need to decide the aim of this advertising campaign because it will cost you; make sure the benefits from advertising exceed the costs. Purposes of ads usually include:

- More Likes: The main purpose here is to increase the number of people who like your page and can potentially share it with friends or family. The concept of strength in numbers is also important because if an existing page has a lot of 'likes' it makes people think it is popular.
- More Fans: This will enable more active participation on your page and you can offer discounts or other deals through ads and even request some of your avid fans to provide testimonials or reviews.

- More Sales: Promoting particular products or posts on your page will create awareness about your product specifications and prices and it will encourage more people to buy.
- More Attendees: If you are organizing an event and the ad caters to that, you want to maximize the number of people who can attend this event and provide some incentive for them if they attend.

Designing the Ad

The next step is to design the ad by selecting various options Facebook presents to you. You can preview the result of each selection to have an idea what your ad would look like. You have to choose to use an external URL by entering it in the field and including other details like the title, image, and main text of your ad.

You can even use your existing Facebook page as a destination. This will highlight any event, post, or other type of activity of your page. In this, you have two further options:

1. Sponsored Story: A story about fans or your page.
    a. Page Like Story: A new user will be shown his or her friend who likes the page, this induces a bandwagon effect because if one or more of a person's close friends like a page it would encourage him to do the same and 'Like' the page.
    b. Page Post Story: A new user will be shown a post or image from your Facebook page in order to spark their interest in the page. The interested user can then 'Like', Comment or Share this story.
2. Facebook Ads: For this, you will need to enter your Facebook page in the Destination tab. You can create the ad using catchy phrases, interesting text and an image, by clicking on the link users will be redirected to your page.

Targeted Ads

You have to be careful about the potential audience of your ad.

Promote your page only where your business actually operates and can deliver products to. The ultimate aim is to increase sales or popularity.

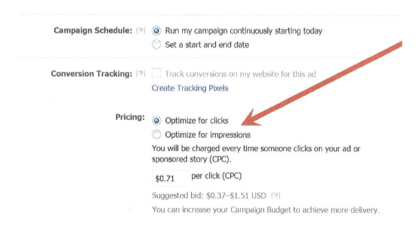

expand

Select a Pricing Plan

You can either pay every time a user clicks on your ad or pay per impression; the latter refers to paying every time a user sees your ad.

Lastly review your ad and place an order for it.

🗪 Review Ads

Review your ads to make sure you're happy with it. The audience for your ads includes people under th reviewed before it's made public on Facebook.

Ad Preview:

Ad Name:

Audience: This ad targets users:
- who live in the United States

Campaign: http://flashingfl...-Clicks-US-13-65 (New Campaign)
Bid Type: CPC
Bid: $0.71 USD per click
Daily Budget: $10.00 USD per day
Duration: This ad campaign will run indefinitely

Place Order   Edit Ad

Place Order   Edit Ad

By clicking the "Place Your Order", I agree to the Facebook Statement of Rights and Responsibilites including my obligation to comply with the Facebook Advertising Guidelines. I understand that failure to comply with the Terms and Conditions and the Advertising Guidelines may result in a variety of consequences including the cancellation of any advertisements I have placed, and termination of my account. I understand that if I am resident or have my principal place of business in the US or Canada, I am contracting solely with Facebook, Inc. Otherwise I am contracting solely with Facebook Ireland Limited.

All Campaigns

Notifications

You don't have any notifications

| Last 28 Days ▼ | All Except Deleted ▼ | Full Report |

Campaign ?	Status ?
Promoting "$1,895,000..."	✓ Completed ▼
Promoting "Fractal 062 Digital Art by Taylor Pam - Fractal..."	✓ Completed ▼
Promoting "407 Beacon Boston, MA : Back Bay 02115 $4,850,000"	✓ Completed ▼
Promoting "Cos 114 Digital Art by Taylor Pam - Cos 114 Fine..."	✓ Completed ▼
Promoting "Enter Innovative Publishers 1st Novel..."	✓ Completed ▼
Promoting "$2700 / 1br - 955ft² - 1 Bd on Tremont St., Avail..."	✓ Completed ▼
Promoting "FREE RENT UNTIL SEPTEMBER 1ST, 2013..."	✓ Completed ▼
Intergalactic Tra...-Post Engagement-US-25-50	✓ Completed ▼
http://store.fast...-Clicks-US-M-26-60	✓ Completed ▼
$hop at Home-Post Engagement-US-26-47	✓ Completed ▼
Innovative Publis...-Post Engagement-US-13-65	✓ Completed ▼
Promoting "Enter Innovative Publishers 1st Novel..."	✓ Completed ▼

CHAPTER 7

Optimize Facebook's Money-Making Potential

Get Customers

The purpose behind acquiring more likes on your Facebook is to fortify your fan base since these fans will translate into customers eventually. Fans could be on the lookout for different offers or discounts and they can make purchases during the lifespan of business. Building a customer base is important because it would directly increase your sales and lead to the expansion of your business. When your fans become your customers it is beneficial in the long run because satisfied customers would tell their relatives or friends about their good experience with your business and this will lead to positive publicity for your brand.

Increasing your customer base is a viable option for Facebook pages because business can become very successful once they develop a loyal and committed clientele. There are several ways to increase the number of customer on your Facebook page. Some of them include:

Discounts: Offering discounts is one way to transform your fans into customers. Those who were not interested in the products or couldn't afford it would now have an option to buy.

Free Delivery: This is an effective way to gather more customers because when buying online it provides them with an additional incentive to order. It is cheaper for them to order things if they can save on the delivery charges. Additionally, the frequency of their orders will also increase if the delivery is free.

Focus on Quality: In addition to increase fans, pay attention towards the number of existing fans that you have. Encourage them to participate in different contests or activities on the Facebook page and you can even award them with gift hampers once in a while.

Pay Attention: If some of your fans interact more on the page then you should always try to feature super fans weekly or monthly so that they can feel recognized for their participation.

Interact: Communicating directly with your potential customers will always be beneficial because it would create a good working relationship. You can ask them to share their photos, personal experiences or even reviews of the product. Encourage users to share your posts and contribute their own constructive criticism on your page.

You can also engage in these strategies to increase customers for your page:

- Make your customers the topic of discussion and try to acknowledge their presence or monumental life events.

  You can even participate with them in national or global events like holidays, charity drives, national games, or even in times of need. As a part of the community you can mobilize your fans to connect in a socially responsible way.
- Rewarding your customers consistently for their participation on the fan page is also very important because it would make them feel like a part of a community. When sending gift hampers to your super fans you should always appreciate them publically through a wall post so that other customers would also know that participation is rewarding.
- If you formulate a strategy where you want to expand your customer base you should always try to make contributions towards it daily. Think about creative ways to engage your fans and devise a schedule for posting updates and conducting contests so that your fans would expect it within

a few months or weeks. This would encourage them to participate whenever there is an event.

Use Facebook EdgeRank to Your Advantage

What is EgdeRank?

EdgeRank is the alogorithm Facebook uses to determine what kinds of posts appear in a person's daily newsfeed. In addition it gives information about where these posts appear. EdgeRank is composed of three components i.e. Affinity, Weight and Time Decay.

http://whatisedgerank.com

Affinity

This refers to the ordinal basis of ranking of posts in the newsfeed based on the relationship of the user to the other person. For example, posts by your family member or close friends are more likely to appear in the top entries of the newsfeed compared to posts by other friends with whom you do not communicate that often. Interacting with someone ensures that their posts appear in your newsfeed; however, the converse is not always true.

Weight

Different types of posts on Facebook carry more weightage compared to others. For instance, photos have the most weight, links have the second highest weight and textual updates have the least weight. The weight also differs if there are more likes or comments attached to it, so a status update with many likes will have more weight compared to a photo with no likes.

Time Decay

Another important component is measuring how old the post is. The frequency with which users check their Facebook page means that posts will decay very fast and it is important to bring up fresh content more rapidly.

Importance of EdgeRank

EdgeRank is important because advertising has to be brought near to consumers on their newsfeed. Users cannot be expected to go back and visit fan pages of different businesses they have liked several months ago. In fact 96% of the fans do not visit the page of the brand after the initial engagement and 27% of user's time on Facebook is spent browsing the newsfeed; therefore, it is important to be in the proximity of your fans.

Strategies to Improve EdgeRank

1. Optimizing the length of your post will be beneficial in most cases because it will allow readers to read and respond quickly. Lengthy posts are rarely well-liked or effective; at least not for brands wanting to sell. Therefore, try to make sure your post stays within the 250 characters limit.

2. Use creative ways to break the monotony of textual communication. Posting photos, infographics, comics, memes or videos are attention grabbing tools get more than 100% engagement on average compared to plain text posts. If you want to redirect users to an informative article try to do so with a photo and give the link in the description.

3. By using interactive posts you will drive more traffic towards your page. Asking questions, allowing users to choose the best answer, asking for their opinion, fill-in-the-blank questions will involve more users.

4. You can ask your fans to go to your page and check the box that says, 'Show in Newsfeed' or 'Get Notifications' this will allow more visibility for your activity on their home page.

5. Increase the frequency with which you post updates so that sooner or later it reaches your fans' newsfeeds.

6. Try to post during the time when most people are active on Facebook. Usually this is the prime time i.e. from 9 pm to 10pm or even midnight.

Lastly, it is important to deliver content that is comprehensive, interesting and appealing so that you do not offend anyone or get hidden from their newsfeed permanently.

CHAPTER 8

Cross-Promote Your Page

Promotion is a continuous and dynamic process which would require you to publicize your brand in every possible formal or informal way. Brand awareness is a cardinal step towards increasing sales and creating a presence in the market. Cross promotion is beneficial because it would increase the popularity of your business and encourage more people to get involved by liking the page. There are many opportunities in the cyberspace to attract new users and to expand your fan base. Cross promotion enables you to look beyond the advertising solutions available on page such as posting better content or making Facebook ads; it ensures that you could indirectly convince more people to become a part of your brand's online community. Some of the ways to achieve this are stated here.

Online Promotion

Online promotion is one of the most effective types of cross promotions because your page is made accessible to millions of people with just a click. You can encourage other businesses or individuals to promote your page by sharing its link on their Facebook pages. Secondly, you can provide a link to your page on your website and on your blog so that users could find you on Facebook. Thirdly, while sending emails or communicating with people try to include your Facebook URL in the footer of the email; this way the reader of the email can easily find out more about your brand by clicking on the link. Fourthly, you should promote your page across different platforms to different types of audiences. For instance, you can even link your Twitter profile to your Facebook page so that your tweets are simultaneously posted on your page and the fan base on Twitter can follow you on Facebook as well. Lastly, when posting on other pages or interacting with people you can always request them to visit your page or check out your content without allowing it to become spam on their newsfeed.

Offline Promotion

Offline promotion can be less extensive but it is still effective. Putting your Facebook page address on your business card, business diaries, calendars or posters will help create awareness of your brand name. If you organize an event you can even put the phrase, 'Find us on Facebook' along with the link on the backdrop or standees so that the people attending can interact with you on Facebook. When making brochures for your company or when designing pamphlets for a conference or annual event you can always include the link to your Facebook page to encourage readers to visit. Offline promotion can also happen through informal means or word of the mouth. You can always encourage your employees or team members to share your page on their personal profiles so that their friends could like the page as well.

In essence cross platform promotion would encourage you to synergize and combine all the resources at your disposal to create awareness for your brand.

Show-off Your Product

While promoting your Facebook page do not digress from the purpose of the page; which is to sell products or services. If you advertise very heavily but the product is of mediocre quality sooner or later you will end up losing your customers. Spending on advertising is only justified if your product is of a good quality otherwise it results as a sunk cost. Most businesses on Facebook have their product catalog available as photographs in various albums and the focus is placed on increasing the product range.

However, if you keep on adding photos to an album you will find that some of the products will not receive that much attention and you won't be able to provide descriptions for every product at once. Since you have to encourage people to buy through words or a photograph at most, you will have to use your resources wisely.

Take Good Photos

If you are advertising a product range make sure that the photographs posted are taken in a proper manner to show all the specifications of the product. You can even take photos from more than one angle to give customers a better perspective. The lighting and editing of the photos should display the product to its advantage.

Provide Descriptions

Invest time in coming up with good descriptions for your product which explain all of its components and give users detailed specifications about it. Think about the different uses of your products and try to advertise the item in the description by using a persuasive tone.

Provide Prices

Even though most firms might not be comfortable with this idea of providing prices with the products it is highly likely that most users will ask you for the prices again and again, if you haven't provided it in the description. You can always modify the prices on a monthly or yearly basis depending on your profit margin but your aim should be to provide the users with complete information so that they can decide autonomously.

Share

If you use albums to catalog your products some of the items might receive less attention, after a week or so share the photo of that item again on your Facebook page so that new users would get an idea about the product. You can also share albums or links on other Facebook pages and on your own wall regularly.

Advertise

You can always use Facebook ads to make sure your products appear in the newsfeed or homepage of new users. If your ad is appealing and targeted towards the right audience your products will receive more attention.

Highlight

On your page you should always post positive reviews, awards, testimonials, endorsements and other sponsorships that you have received from external audiences. If you use high quality materials in your product or if you provide special offers like free delivery, make sure these are properly publicized with every product you advertise. You can even highlight 'product of the month' or 'highest selling products' on your page too.

Fine-Tuned Targeting

While advertising on Facebook, the information about your brand or products will be available to a large number of people who might not even belong to your target audience. For instance, someone who lives in an area where your business does not deliver, these fans are not entirely useless but the probability of them becoming a customer in the near future is very low. Therefore, you might have to fine tune the targeting of your customers.

There are several ways to do this:

Location: While making ads make sure you select the geographical location of the audience where your business operates. For instance, if you sell cakes in a particular city you interest should be in advertising to the residents of that city alone. National or international advertisement is wasteful because cakes are perishable.

Age: Similarly, when selecting the age appropriate for your posts try to target the right demographic. Teenagers might not be interested in buying furniture or ordering home appliances, while adults might not be too keen on purchasing pop art or other fashion accessories.

Gender: In the same way, select the gender of your audience wisely. If you sell women's lingerie your ads should be geared towards attracted females only because they are more likely to buy such items. Beauty products, clothes and shoes designed specifically for women should be advertised only to them.

Interests: Find people with similar interests, lifestyles or hobbies so that you can advertise your product on their home page. For instance, a girl who has liked several fashion pages might be interested in a jewelry shop too. Similarly, if you are selling guns or spare parts of a car try to focus on male audiences. You can streamline your audience by focusing on their jobs, education, activities or other interests.

Existing Fans: Try to advertise to your existing fan base by understanding their requirements or demand and by offering products or services they might be interested in. For instance, if you lose sales through high prices on your products try to offer discount prices for a limited time to encourage sales and to target those people who cannot afford the product at the original price. Try to create more fan engagement and focus on friends of these fans who could potentially become your fans.

Mobile Users: You can even fine tune your target market by improving the way ads are displayed for mobile and tablet users. For this you will have to download and install Power Editor to test different types of ad placements for mobile users. Usually placing the ad in the newsfeed allows you to target a wider audience.

Broad Categories: Facebook will also provide you with broad categories you can directly advertise to. The audiences are formed after Facebook analyzes their activities and interests. Some of the categories include small business owners, football fans, Asians, engaged; have a birthday coming up and so on. If your business sells football jerseys then you might be interested in targeting the 'football fan' category.

You can use other categories like languages, relationship status, education or workplace to further fine tune your target audience so that your advertising budget is spent wisely.

Keep Updating

The key to having a successful Facebook page is to provide the latest information to all users. Some fans are old while some are new, the information dissemination through your updates should be such that everyone one has a basic awareness of your product range, special services, and prices, so that even if they don't buy anything themselves they can always recommend to page to another friend who might be interested in it. For restaurants, beauty parlors, clothes retailers, and other such businesses it is always important to provide accurate and up-to-date information about the location, phone number, discount offers and prices of the products. It will be an unwelcome surprise for clients if your Facebook page does not follow the rules of your business outlet.

Similarly, the information you share must be verified so that users do not end up making wrong decisions. Any facts, upcoming events or offers should be in perfect synchronicity with your business plan. If you are no longer offering a discount, remove the offer from your page, or let the fans to know if it has expired. In the same vein if you no longer have a product available then remove it from the catalog; if you still take orders mention that in the description.

New fans on your page will rarely go through all the posts on your timeline; so any long-standing offers or ads should be reposted often so that all users become aware of it. As mentioned earlier, time decay is an important part in decreasing visibility for the posts, if your posts are new and updated frequently they will have better chance of appearing in the user's newsfeed. Instead of wasting time on rewriting similar posts, share the existing posts on your timeline for new users.

The integration of your business ideology with your Facebook page, as well as the act of following through different plans and strategies, will ensure the success of your business in the long run.

Facebook Help Developer Tools

The use of Facebook developer tools can also help you fine-tune your target audience. The "Custom Audience Targeting" tool makes it possible for you to target your ad to a specific group of users. These users may be those with whom you already have an established relationship on or off the Facebook platform. The audiences can defined through Facebook UIDs, email addresses, phone numbers, Apple's IDFA or app user IDs.

The "Lookalike audiences" tool is also great for targeting the audience that look like they could be your potential customers. It can be used to target people with similar interests and who are like your current group of existing customers. The "lookalike audiences" option can also be optimized for effectiveness. You can optimize for similarity or optimize for greater reach. Optimizing for similarity enables Facebook to locate the visitors that are similar to the existing audience. Though the range of its reach is not that vast, it is specific. On the other hand, optimizing for greater reach will allow you to reach out to similar audiences but with less focus on precision. Therefore you will target a greater audienc

Design Vendors

dsgn.io

I am a proud lefty, Aries, and space bandit. The only pencil I trust is a Ticonderoga. I was born on Easter Sunday, 1988. I used to be an "Army-brat". My parents despised video games while I was growing up, so I am making up for it now (3DS, what's up?). I make music under various aliases, the most common being "the Wibby" (also FRSH×BTS and Spaceman Fresh).

I named my portfolio "Design Services for the Good Natured" because no one likes a jerk. Every day brings about new opportunities, inspiration, and kick-ass "whoah" moments. Spread the love and do your part by inspiring others as you've been inspired! (: That's what I try to do anyway.

https://twitter.com/NetOpWibby

http://dribbble.com/nokadota

Follow the companies and products showcased in this book:

GROUPGLOBAL.NET
http://groupglobal.net/
http://www.facebook.com/cybershoptoday
- Office products, home and gift accessories

Global Realty & Investment Corp
http://gric-ma.com
https://www.facebook.com/globalrealtyinvestment
- Real estate sales and service

Intergalactic Travel Authority
http://ita-travelauthority.com/
https://www.facebook.com/intergalacticauthority
- Travel agent and accomodations

Innovative Publishers Inc.
http://publishing-universe.com
https://www.facebook.com/InnovativePublishers
- Book and magazine publisher

Boston School of Real Estate Inc.
http://boston-realestateschool.com
https://www.facebook.com/Boston.RealEstateSchool
- Real estate school

Taylor Pam – Fine Art LLC
http://taylorpam.com
https://www.facebook.com/taylorpam.fineartist
- Digital, acrylic and oil paintings

Love is... https://www.facebook.com/loveis.sdwebb
- Author (Love is...) and entrepreneur

How to increase sales using Pinterest
https://www.facebook.com/sellonpinterest
- Social media marketing for businesses

How to increase sales using Facebook
https://www.facebook.com/sellonline1
- Social media marketing for businesses

Trademark Disclaimer

Product names, logos, brands and other trademarks referred to within Innovative Publishers Inc.'s publications products and services and within innovative-publishers.com are the property of their respective trademark holders. These trademark holders are not affiliated with Innovative Publishers Inc., our products, or our website. They do not sponsor or endorse our materials.

All trademarks remain property of their respective holders, and are used only to directly describe the products being provided. Their use in no way indicates any relationship between Twisted Lincoln, Inc. and the holders of said trademarks.

Innovative Publishers

Double Click Press

Document your progress

Project Plan

Title

Outcome

Start Date

Completion Date

Notes

Project Plans

Notes

Project Name

Title

Outcome

Start Date

Completion Date

Notes

Project Plans

Notes

Title

Outcome

Start Date

Completion Date

Notes

Project Plans

Notes

Project Plan

Title

Outcome

Start Date		Completion Date

Notes

Project Plans

Notes

Project Plans

Title

Outcome

Start Date

Completion Date

Notes

Project Plans

Notes

Project Plans

Title

Outcome

Start Date

Completion Date

Notes

Project Plans

Notes

Project Plans

Title

Outcome

Start Date

Completion Date

Notes

Project Plans

Notes

Project Plans

Title

Outcome

Start Date

Completion Date

Notes

Project Plans

Notes

Project Name

Title

Outcome

Start Date

Completion Date

Notes

Project Plans

Notes

Project Plan

Title

Outcome

Start Date

Completion Date

Notes

Project Plans _____

Notes

Project Plans

Title

Outcome

Start Date	Completion Date

Notes

Project Plans

Notes

Project Plans

Title

Outcome

Start Date

Completion Date

Notes

Project Plans

Notes

Title

Outcome

Start Date

Completion Date

Notes

Project Plans

Notes

Project Plans

Title

Outcome

Start Date

Completion Date

Notes

Project Plans

Notes

Project Name

Title

Outcome

Start Date	Completion Date

Notes

Project Plans

Notes

Project Plans

Title

Outcome

Start Date

Completion Date

Notes

Project Plans

Notes

Project Plans

Title

Outcome

Start Date	Completion Date

Notes

Project Plans

Notes

Project Plans

Title

Outcome

Start Date	Completion Date

Notes

Project Plans

Notes

Project Plans

Title

Outcome

Start Date

Completion Date

Notes

Project Plans

Notes

www.ingramcontent.com/pod-product-compliance
Lightning Source LLC
Chambersburg PA
CBHW041141050326
40689CB00001B/444